Avgusta Udartseva

7 Versions Passacaglia – Handel / Halvorsen

Piano Sheet Music
from Beginner to Advanced.
With Online Audio

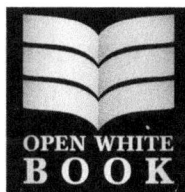

OPEN WHITE
B O O K

ISBN: 978-1-962612-15-9

Messages about typos, errors, inaccuracies and suggestions for
improving the quality are gratefully received at:
avgustaudartseva@gmail.com

CONTENTS

Remember:

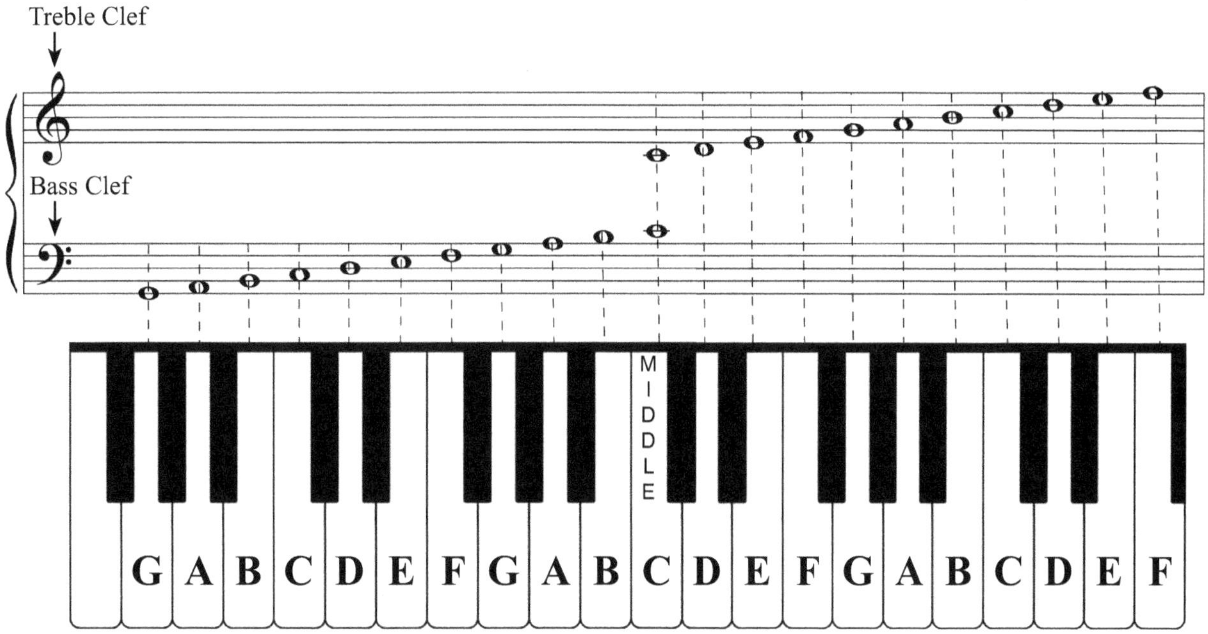

Passacaglia

G. F. Handel / J. Halvorsen

*

C C B C   A C G C   F C E C   D C C C

B B A B   G B F B   E B D B   C B B B

A A G A   F A E A   D A C A   B A A A

A   G♯ F♯   G♯   A   A

*See page 30 for all videos and audio files.

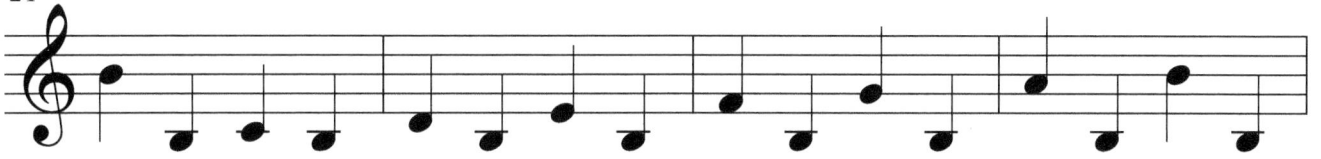

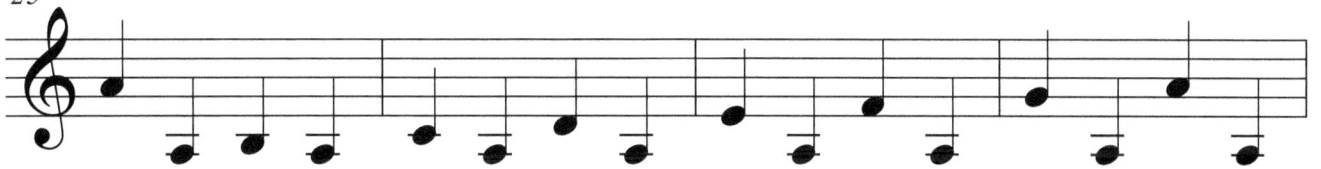

Passacaglia

G. F. Handel / J. Halvorsen

Easy - Version 2

1.
1	5	4	5	3	5	2	5
C	C	B	C	A	C	G	C

2.
1	5	1	5	1	5	1	5
F	C	E	C	D	C	C	C

3.
1	5	4	5	3	5	2	5
B	B	A	B	G	B	F	B

4.
1	5	1	5	1	5	1	5
E	B	D	B	C	B	B	B

5.
1	5	4	5	3	5	2	5
A	A	G	A	F	A	E	A

6.
1	5	1	5	1	5	1	5
D	A	C	A	B	A	A	A

8

7
5 3 2 4
A G♯ F♯ G♯ A A
9
5 1 2 1 3 1 4 1
C C D C E C F C
10
5 1 5 1 5 1 5 1
G C A C B C C C
11
5 1 2 1 3 1 4 1
B B C B D B E B
12
5 1 5 1 5 1 5 1
F B G B A B B B
13
5 1 2 1 3 1 4 1 5 1 5 1 5 1 5 1
A A B A C A D A E A F A G A A A
15
5 3 4
A G♯ F♯ G♯ A A

Passacaglia

G. F. Handel / J. Halvorsen

8
1 5 1 5 1 5 1 5 5 3 2 4
D A C A B A A A A G# F# G# A A
D A F E B G# A E C
11
5 1 2 1 3 1 4 1 5 1 5 1 5 1 5 1
C C D C E C F C G C A C B C C C
A E C D A F
13
5 1 2 1 3 1 4 1 5 1 5 1 5 1 5 1
B B C B D B E B F B G B A B B B
G D B C G E

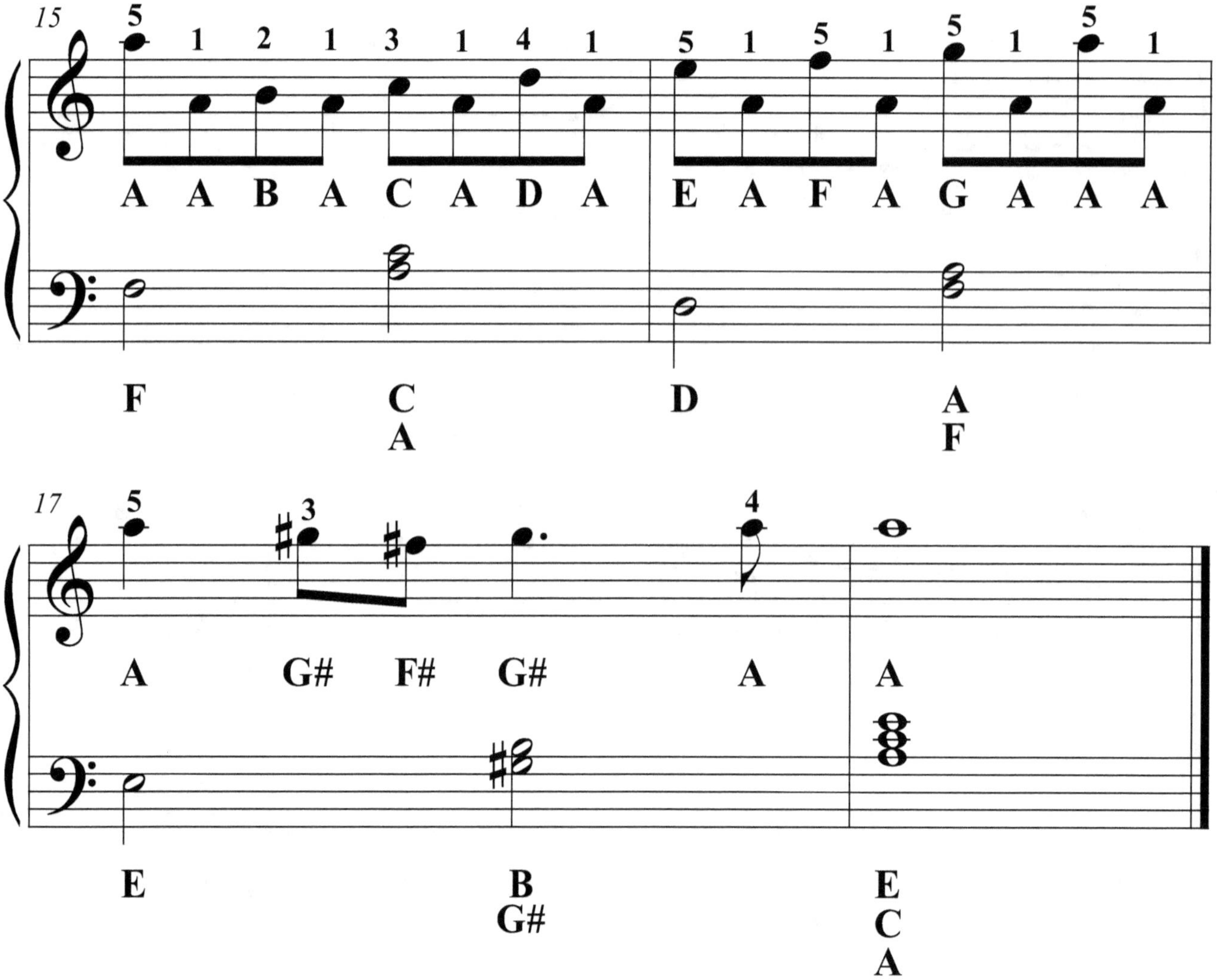
15
5 1 2 1 3 1 4 1 5 1 5 1 5 1 5 1
A A B A C A D A E A F A G A A A
F C A D A F
17
5 3 4
A G# F# G# A A
E B G# E C A

Passacaglia

G. F. Handel / J. Halvorsen

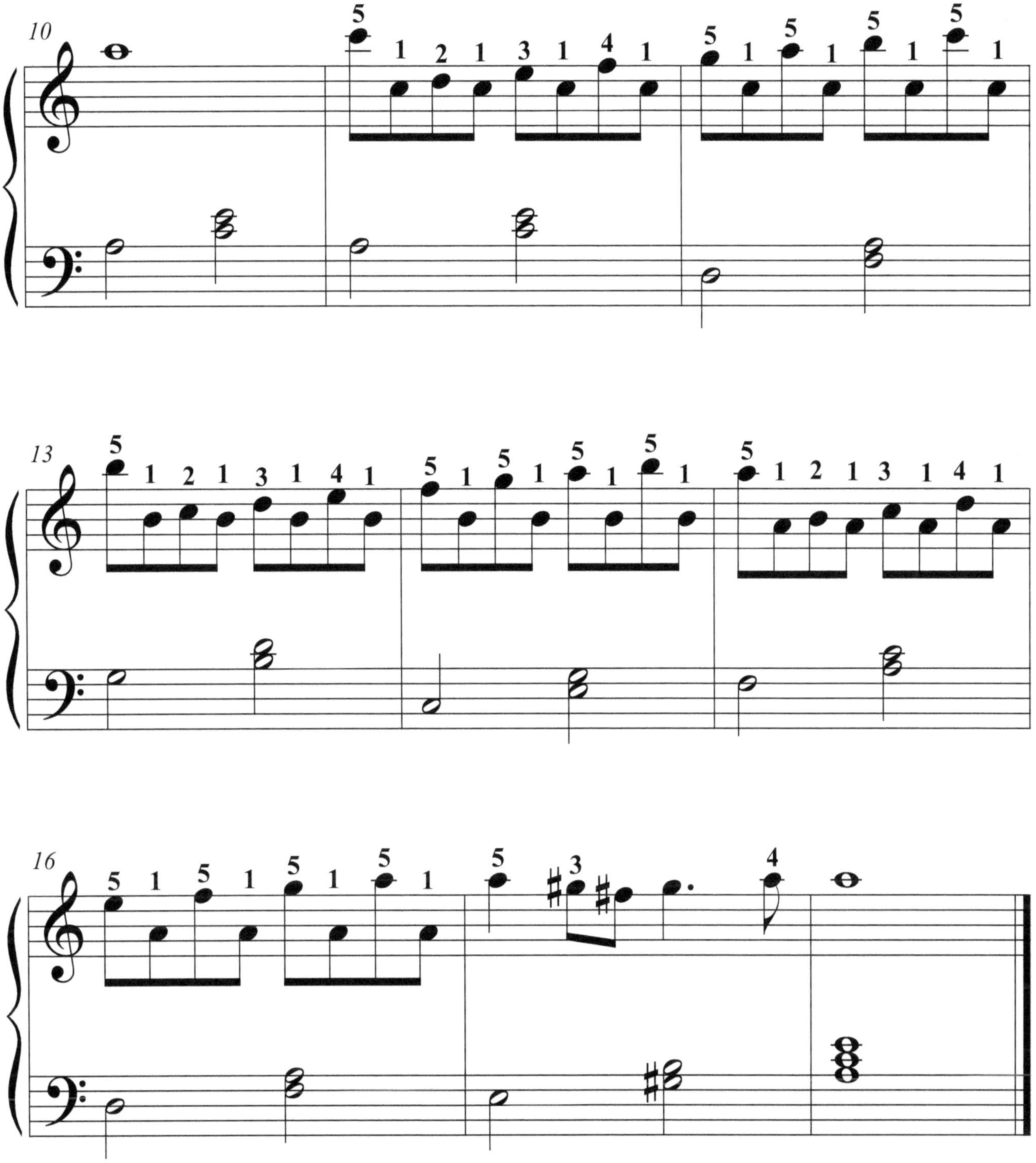
10
13
16

Passacaglia

G. F. Handel / J. Halvorsen

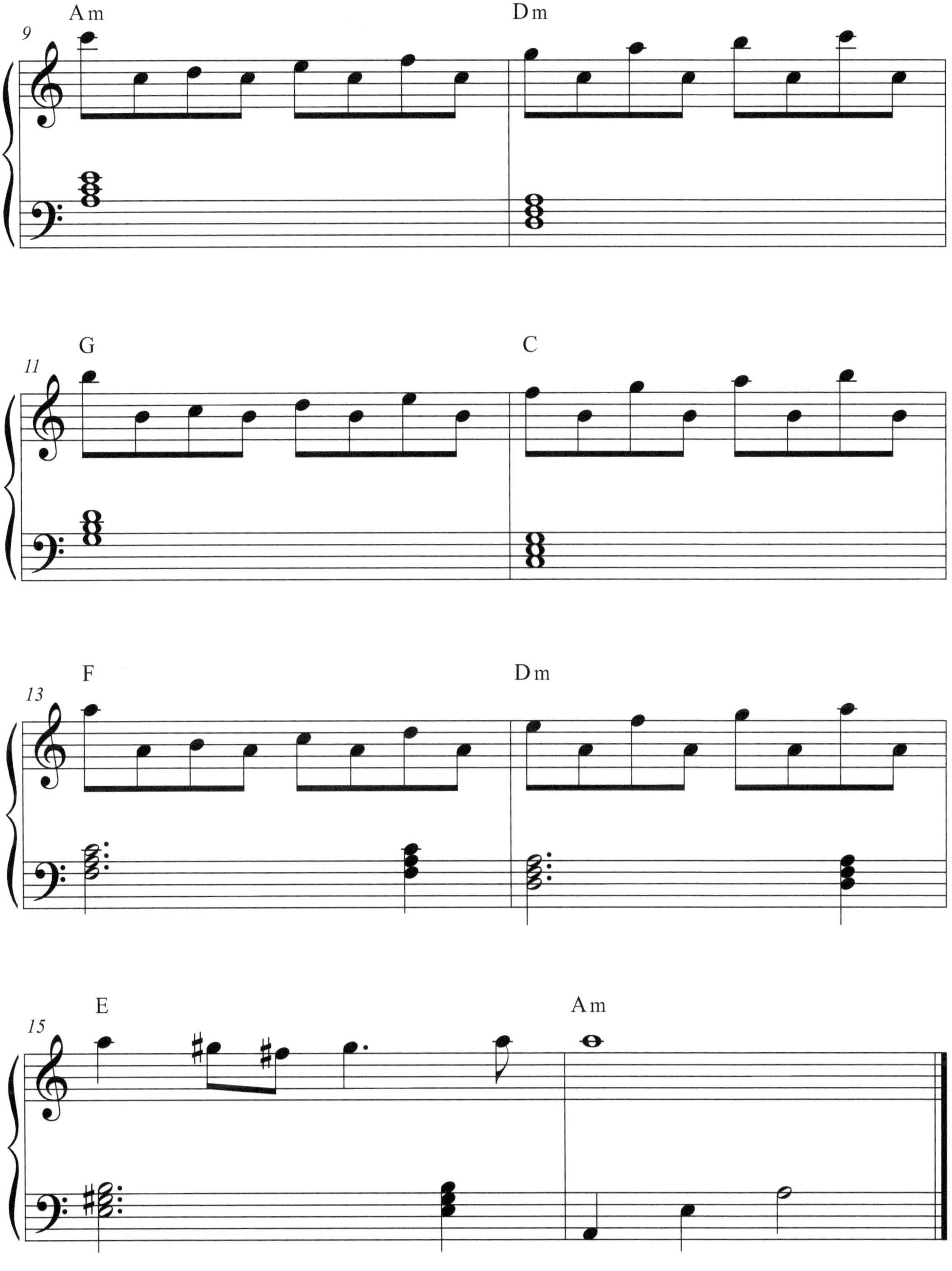
9
Am
Dm
11
G
C
13
F
Dm
15
E
Am

Passacaglia

G. F. Handel / J. Halvorsen

Advanced - Version 5

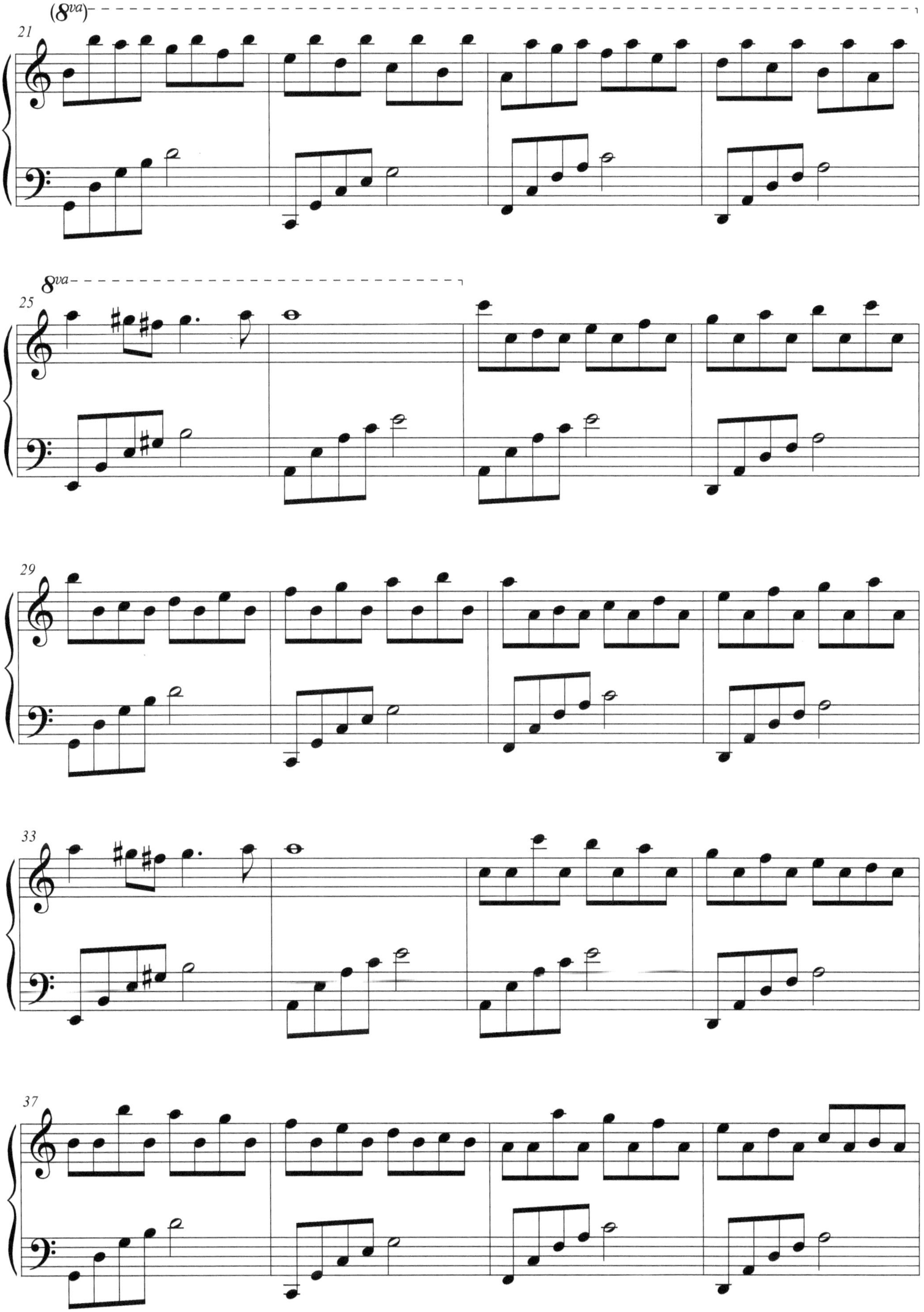
(8va)
21
8va
25
29
33
37

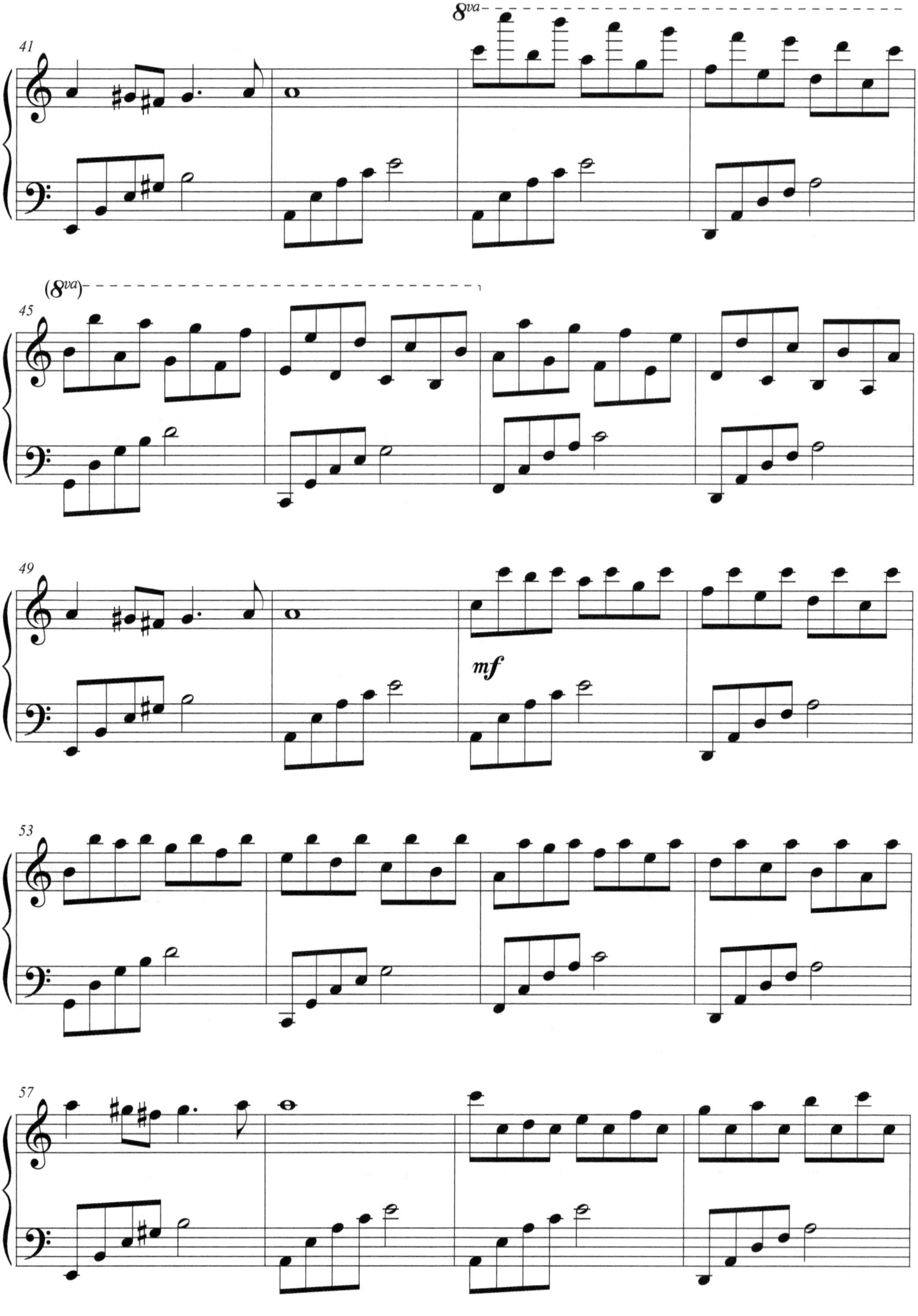
41
8va
45
(8va)
49
mf
53
57

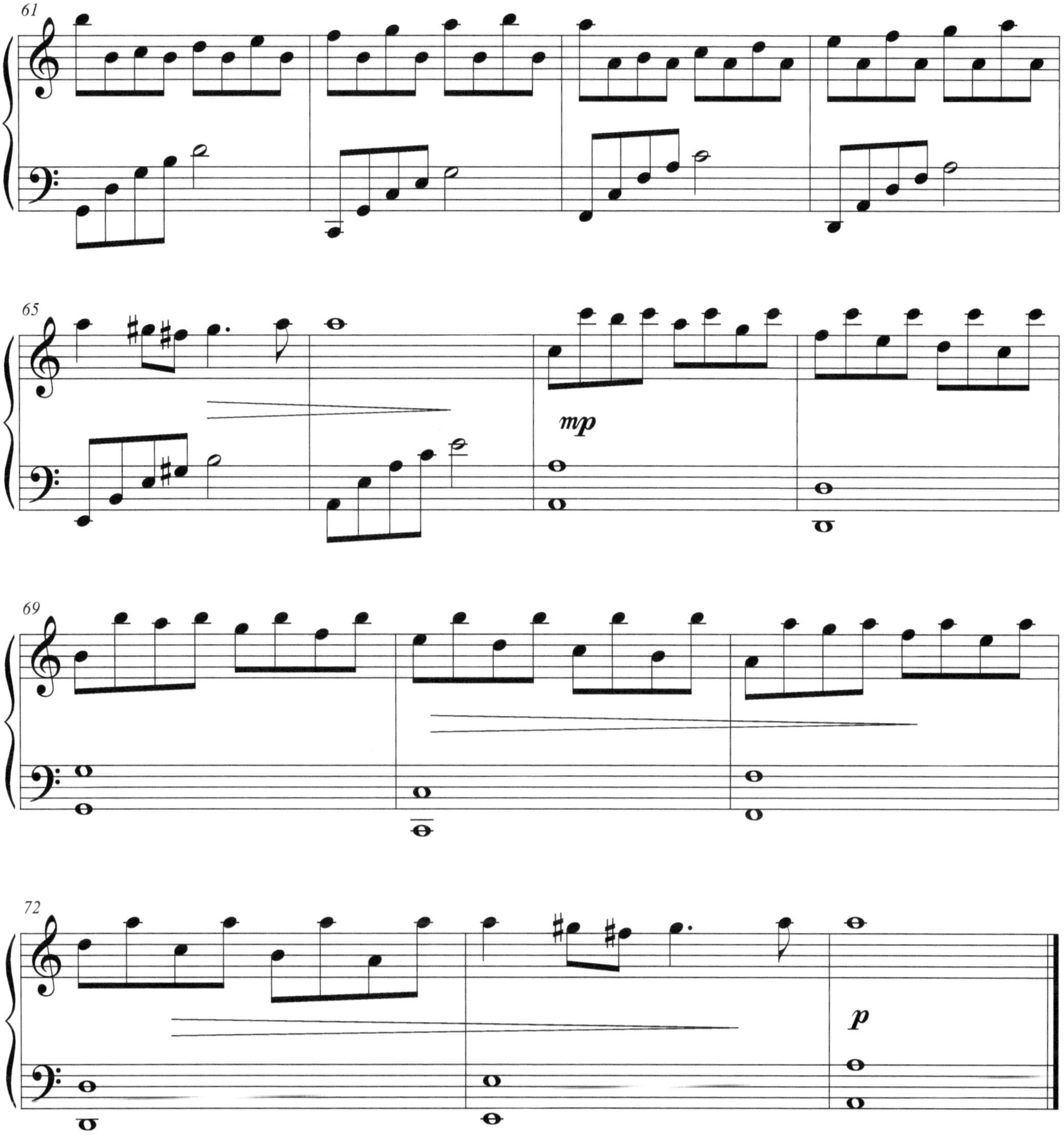
61
65
mp
69
72
p

Passacaglia

G. F. Handel / J. Halvorsen

Advanced - Version 6

Allegro

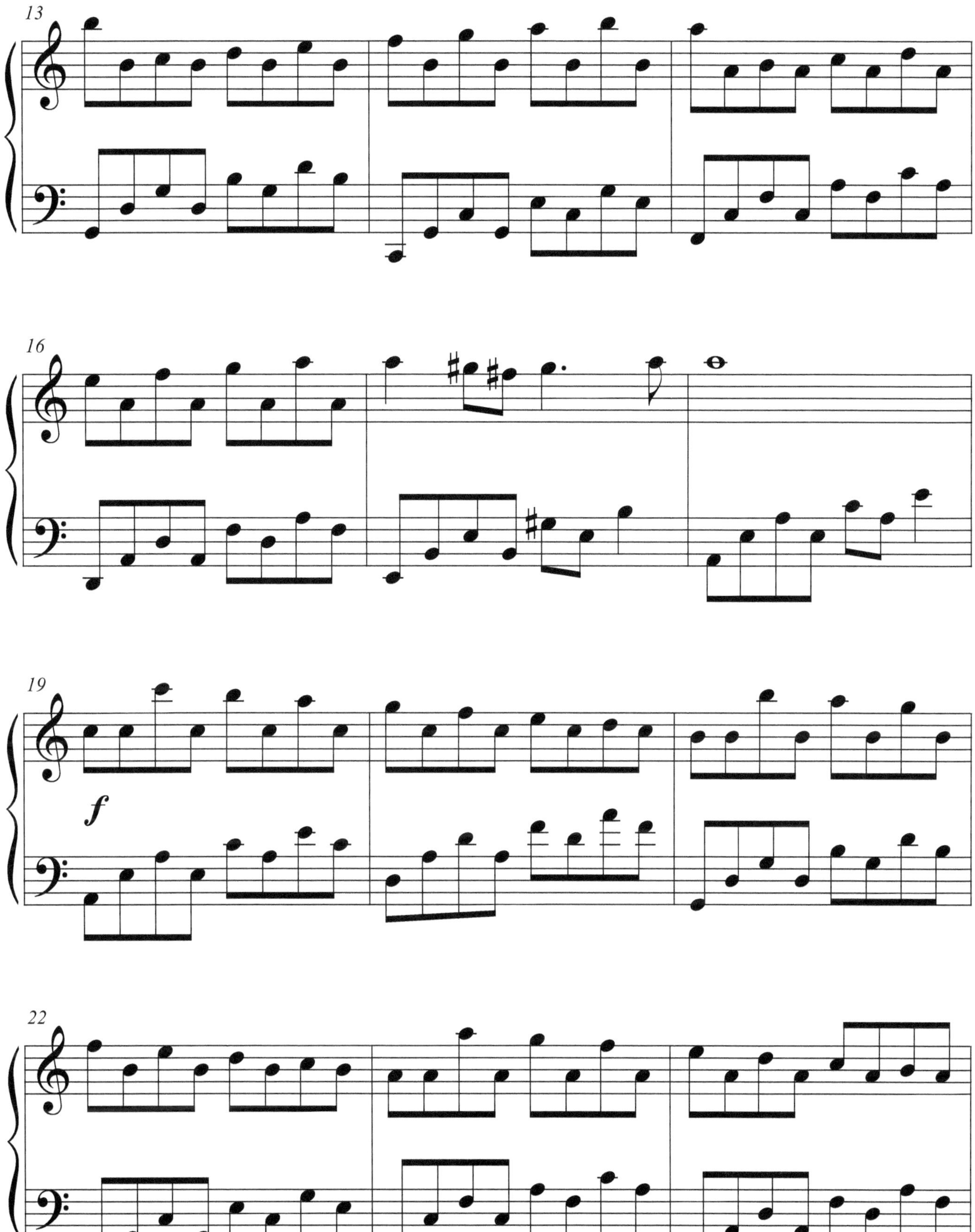
13
16
19
f
22

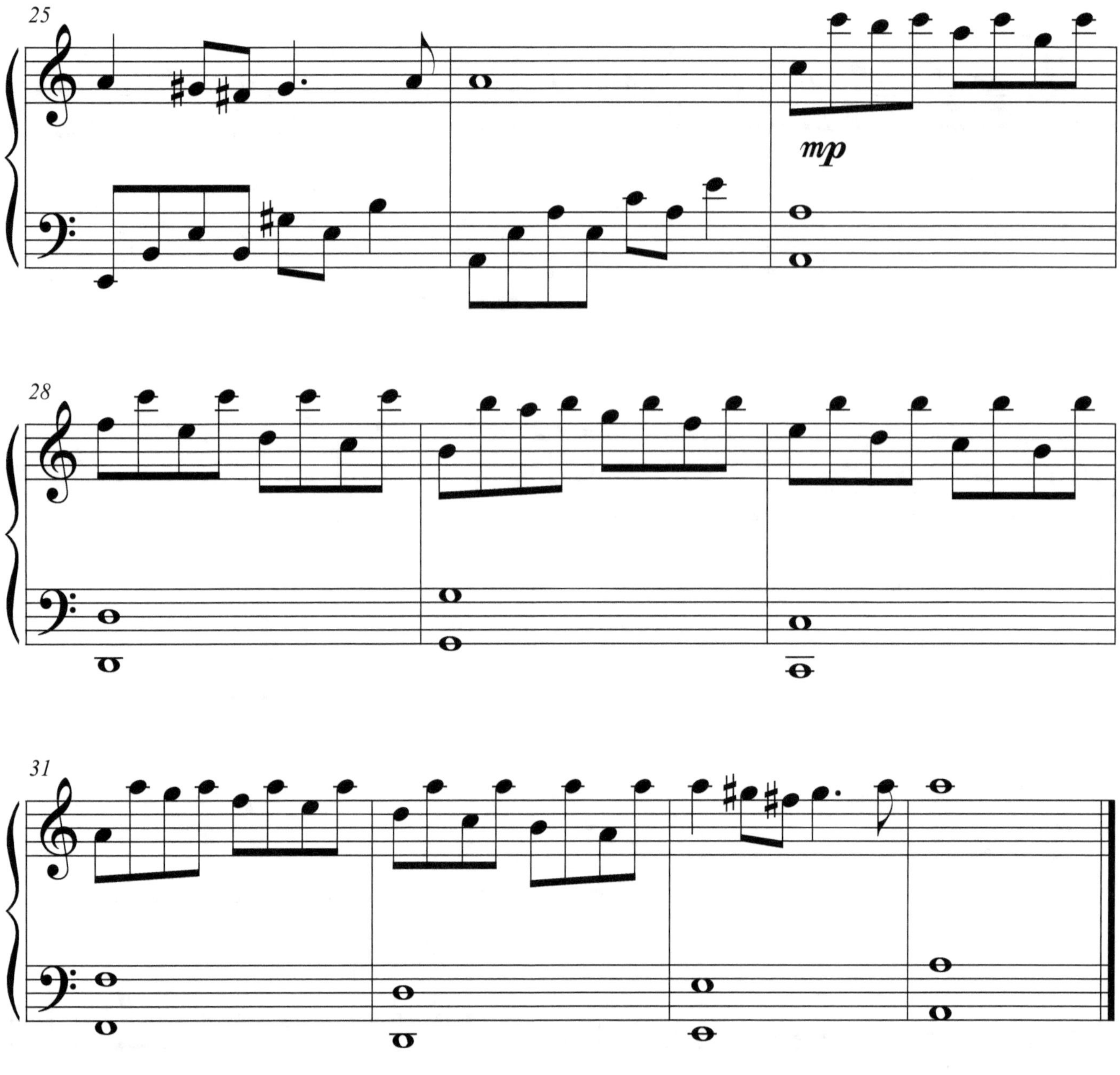
25
mp
28
31

Passacaglia

Original Piece - Version 7

G. F. Handel / J. Halvorsen

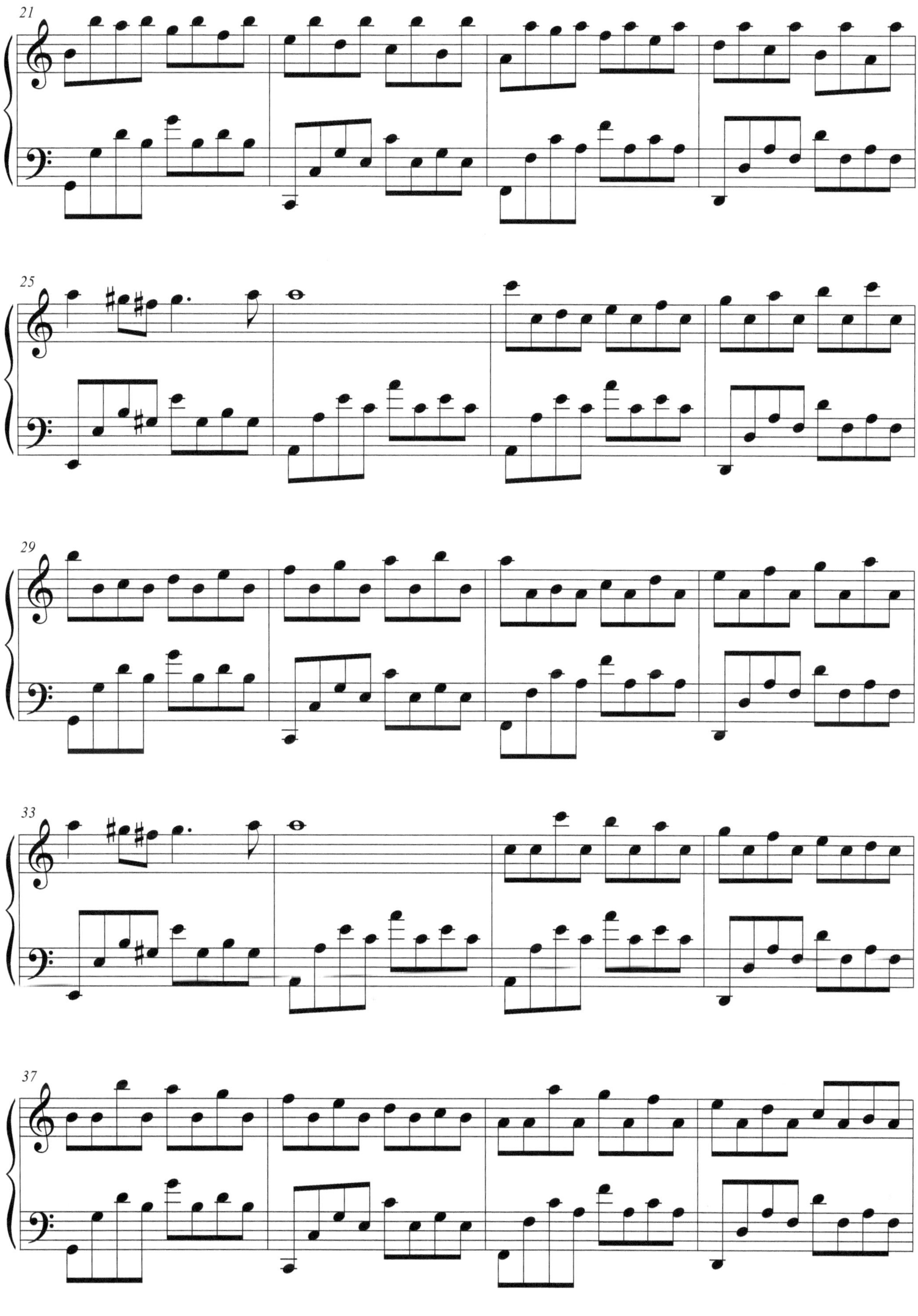
21
25
29
33
37

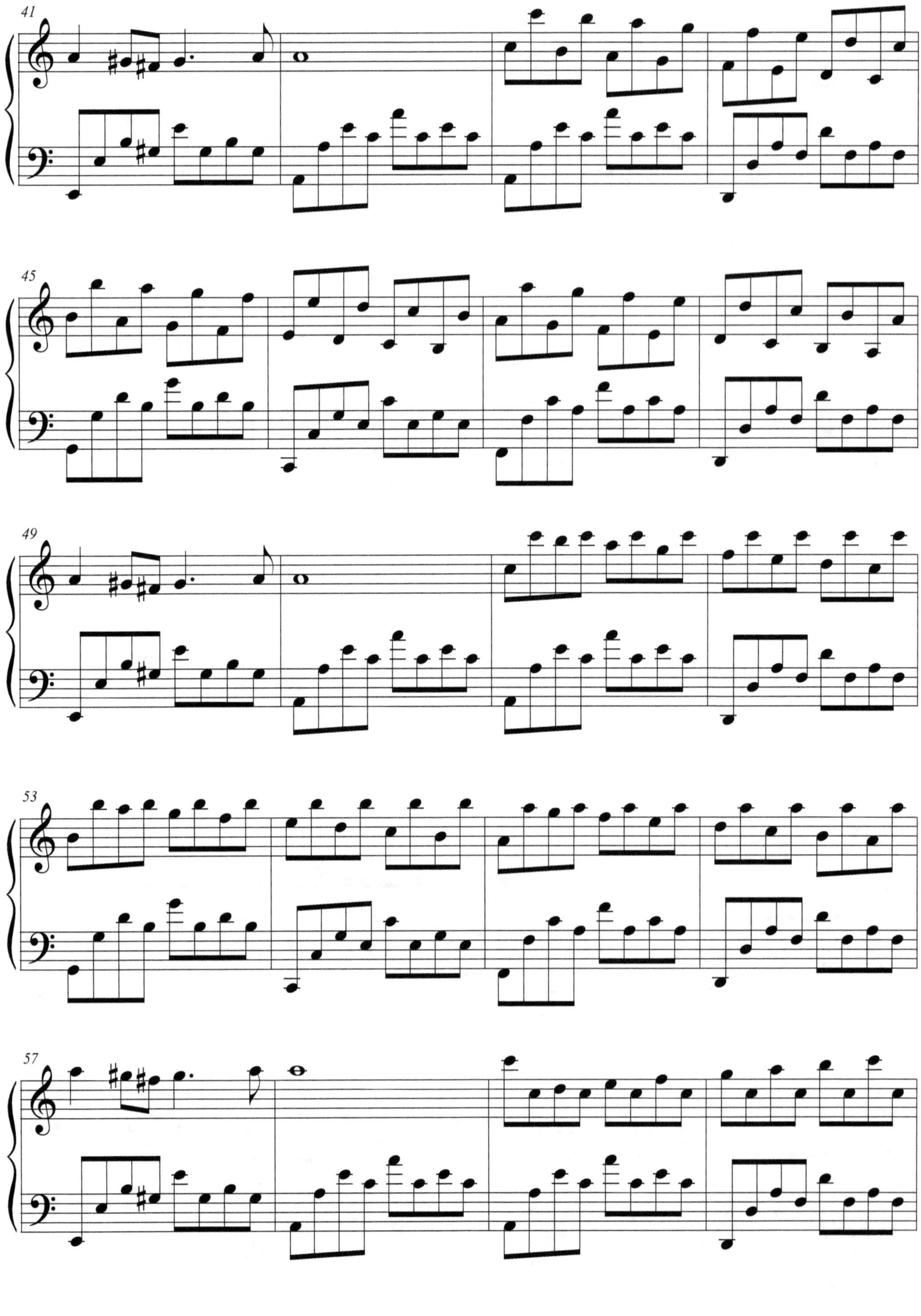
41
45
49
53
57

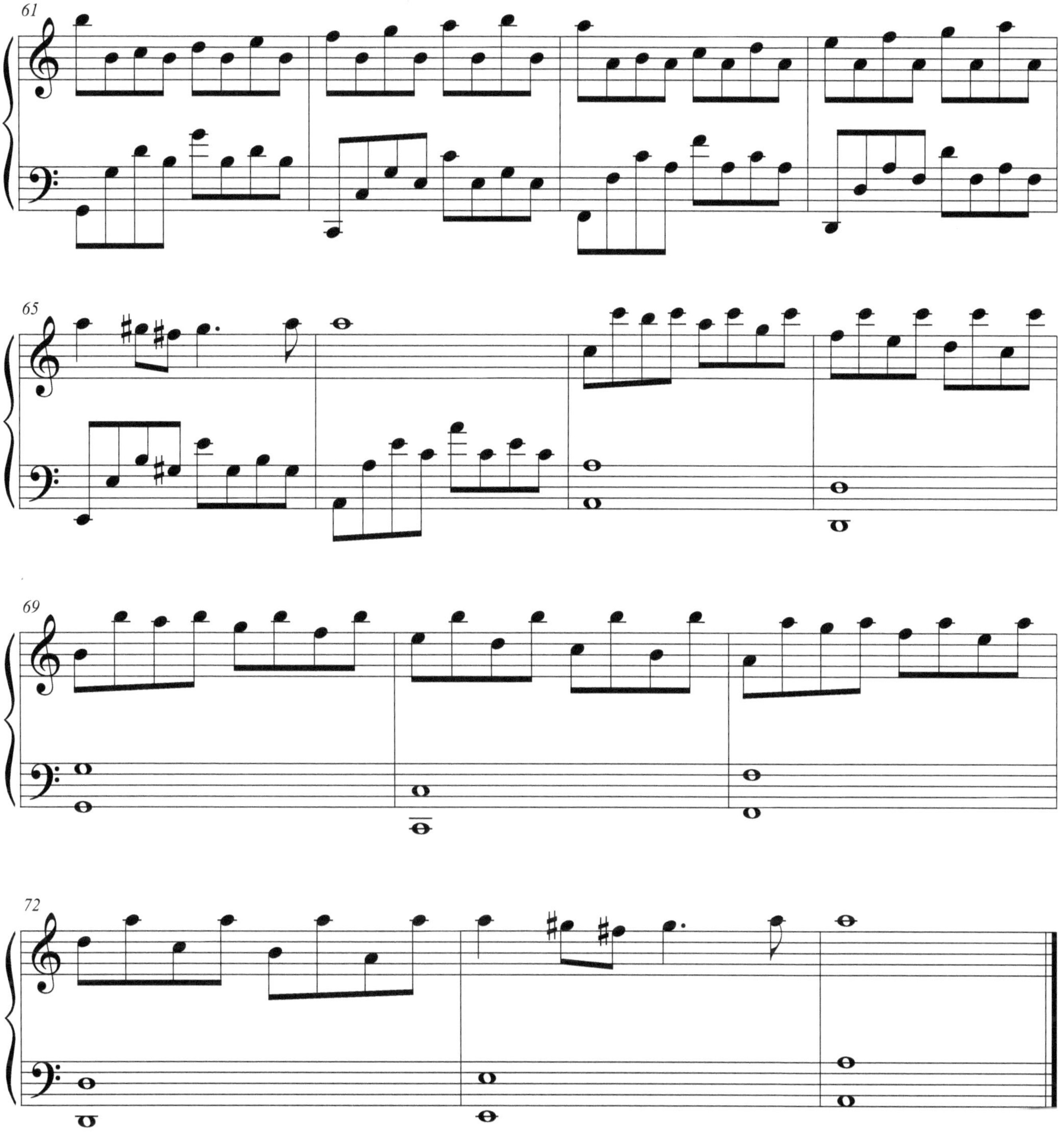
61
65
69
72

All Audio and Video Files for Downloading

All of the audio and video files are also available on Google Drive:

or use the link:

cutt.ly/OeZD5ef9

Important! Be sure to download all files from Google Drive to your computer. We did have a glitch in our system once and our files were temporarily unavailable online. It would be best to download them all at once so you have offline access to them anytime.

For any questions, comments or suggestions, email us at:
avgustaudartseva@gmail.com

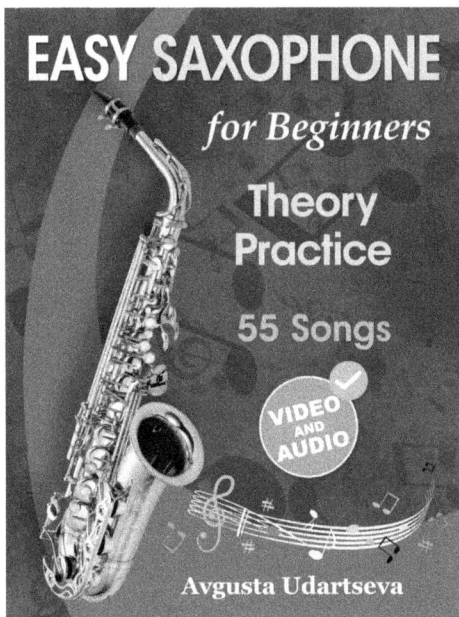

Easy Saxophone for Beginners: Theory, Practice and 55 Songs. For Kids 12+ and Adults. With Online Video and Audio

Complete saxophone instruction book for beginners. For kids 12+ and adults.

This step-by-step guide is for anyone who wants to master the instrument and learn to play their favorite songs effortlessly. The book is also for those who want to learn to swing, play the blues and practice improvisation.

ISBN: 978-1962612098

ASIN: 1962612090

United States   United Kingdom   Canada

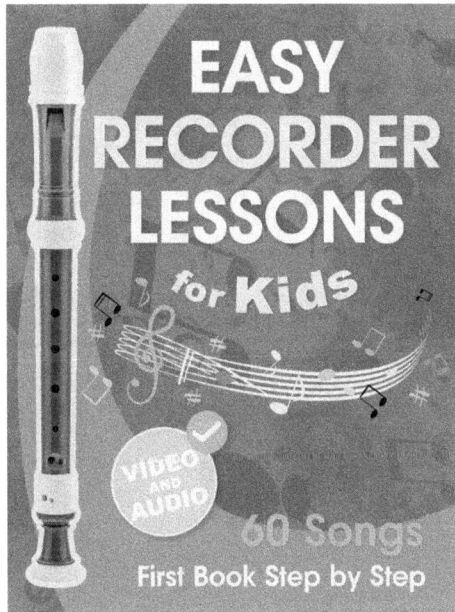

Easy Recorder Lessons for Kids + Video and Audio: Beginner Recorder for Children and Teens with 60 Songs. First Book Step by Step

- Learn the position of the body and hands, how to breathe properly and play easily;
- Letters above each note and simple explanations;
- Convenient large US Letter print size;
- Video accompaniment to all lessons by direct link inside the book;
- 2-in-1 Book: Recorder lessons and video + 60 Songs.

ISBN: 979-8386419004

ASIN: B0BXMX7ZVN

United States   United Kingdom   Canada

And it's great for adults

www.ingramcontent.com/pod-product-compliance
Lightning Source LLC
LaVergne TN
LVHW081337060426
835513LV00014B/1332